Brown Sugar Skin

Tharani Balachandran

Published by Garden of Neuro Publishing
A Division of the Garden of Neuro Institute
Poughkeepsie, New York
www.gardenofneuropublishing.com
Copyright © Tharani Balachandran

ISBN978-1-962077-05-7
Ebook ISBN 978-1-962077-10-1
Cover art: Colin Groves

For Colin and Selvi,
for creating the only love story
I want to be a part of.

Table of Contents

In this house we don't say I love you.......................1

Summer with my cousins, Scarborough (1992).....3

There is no mental illness in our family..................5

Questionnaire for Potential Future Partners 6

No one I love was born in Canada..........................8

If you ask me if I'm fluent in Tamil 10

Late...12

Some things are out of place 14

Lately, I have been contemplating marriage 16

Instructions to ChatGPT in the year 2043...........17

How to romance yourself 19

Untitled...21

What I did today instead of writing a poem 22

A crown of sonnets for what to expect when
you're expecting...24

Five haiku 26

Acknowledgements...27

In this house we don't say I love you

even though there are six words for love in Tamil.

Instead we say,
சாப்பிட்டாயா
We say, *have you eaten?*
We say, *I'll make you a plate.*
We say, *how's the food?*
We say, *you look thin.*
We say, *you've gained weight.*
We say, *how are your studies?*
We say, *how is Amma?*
We say, *do you have a boyfriend yet?*

We say, சரி

We say, *okay.*

We slice a plate of fruit.
We double-bag leftovers for you.
We slip 50 dollars in your back pocket.
We drive you to the airport.
We pack you a snack for the plane.
Even though we know it might be years before we
see you again.
Even though we know we will never see you again
we don't say goodbye.

We say,

போயிட்டு வாங்கோ

We say, *come back soon.*

We say,

போயிட்டு வர்றன்

We say, *I'll come back soon.*

Summer with my cousins, Scarborough (1992)

My sisters and I are lounging through
a hot summer with our cousins in the suburbs.
We ignore the sunshine outside
and hole up in the basement,
eating popsicles and playing cards
and waiting to be fed.
At breakfast,
my grandfather eats Froot Loops with me.
I stare into the bowl and think about how
his brittle nails look like the cereal.
My aunts take their pills, one by one;
blue and white, red and green,
they look like candy.
To my seven-year-old brain
there are hundreds of them, maybe thousands,
too many to count.
In the afternoon,
my mother makes batches of our favorite snack,
skinny coils of deep-fried dough spiced delicately
with coriander and cumin seeds
that we just can't get enough of.
At dinner, my cousins fight over
who gets to eat the fish's eye
because our parents tell us it will make us smarter.
I look at the fish head lying on the table
and decide that I am smart enough.
My aunt supervises me eating
with a wooden spoon at the ready.
My mother tells her, *we don't hit children who don't eat*
but she doesn't need to worry about me here.

At home, I am a picky eater, only white bread
sugar sandwiches and Kraft Dinner
but here I will eat everything my aunts cook,
no matter how spicy it is
or what it looks like: everything is delicious.
Our visits are all snacks and laughter.
My father finds my cousin's scrunchie
between the couch cushions
and says, *here you go, I found your munchie*
and we laugh
until happy tears roll down our cheeks.
This is before,
when I was the only one allowed to laugh
at my parents.
Before anyone at school tells me
that my favorite snack looks like worms.
Before my grandfather dies
and I see my father cry for the first time.

There is no mental illness in our family

Dark skin is supposed to protect you
from sunburns
and mental illness.
My mother is so proud of me when I tell her
it has been months
since I last took my medication.
She says that my anxiety is not a badge to wear.
It is not my identity.
It is not something I earned.
It is not something to brag about.
She is not wrong
but she is still the one who called the ambulance,
rode in the front with the driver,
held my hand
while we walked to the hospital entrance
opposite from the entrance
she normally goes into work.
While we sat for 8 hours in the emergency room
waiting for someone to tell me
what she already knew,
that I was fine,
we made a pact.
I would work harder.
I would stay calmer.
And the next time I stopped breathing,
I would stop wondering if I was happy
and I would just try to sleep.

Questionnaire for Potential Future Partners
after Rachel Wiley

Did you cry when you watched the Notebook?
How many women have you believed?
Do you believe that boys will be boys?
When's the last time you called your mother?
Would you be ashamed if she read your tweets?
How long would you mourn me after I die?
Have you ever had a mullet?
Are you business in front of coworkers and a
party at the back of the bar?
How many times in a row do you sneeze?
Do you prefer cats or dogs?
Are you allergic to cats?
On a scale of tolerate to lay down and die,
how much do you love cats?

Have you ever ghosted anyone?
Do you continue to haunt them?
If I tell you the thing I'm most ashamed of
about myself, will you:
(a) run;
(b) bring it up during every argument we have; or
(c) love me anyway.

How long can you hold a grudge for?
Will you ever hold our relationship hostage?
Will I be able to afford the ransom?
Do you believe that
a woman's temple gives her the right to choose?

Do you listen to Frank Ocean?
Do you listen to the Pacific Ocean?
How did your last relationship end?
How will this one end?

No one I love was born in Canada

Your photo, on the front page of the newspaper,
walking from a ship, with
Is this the face of terrorism? underneath.
A question and pronouncement.

I recognize you immediately.
A sudden breeze in the oppressive heat.
Sweet afternoon tea.
An unpredictable ocean.
Your face,
a home I didn't grow up in.

The ship looms behind you
like an overly protective mother.
She urges you to remain safely
in her soft, iron belly,
stay in the embrace of her supportive steel arms,
but you have outgrown her.
She waits nervously as you step with purpose
into your new home.
Like you, she should not have made it
but she is here anyway.
She lingers in the harbour
like a hesitant parent, watching from the porch,
wondering if you will run back
or wave,
and tell her she can go.

A roped walkway guides you from ship to safety,
The ground unexpectedly steady and hopeful
after your shaky journey.
The air feels deliciously cool on your damp skin.

You hear soothing sounds
gentler than rifles, maybe someone humming
the strains of your favourite film song.
Something smells more alive than the earth.
The person coming towards you isn't smiling.
He is speaking a language
that you can't quite remember.

I wish I had been there to meet you
in the photo, at the end of the walkway,
arms outstretched.
As if we were in an airport.
As if your flight had been delayed
and I had been waiting for you for hours.

If you ask me if I'm fluent in Tamil
after Melissa Lozada-Olivia

I will tell you that I can always tell
when my mother is angry.
I know how to fetch the broom and shoo the cat
but don't have any words to describe my father
staying up all night worrying about the orphaned
baby rabbits he found in the backyard.

My Tamil complains about anything
on a report card that isn't an A.
Tamil is an itch that won't be satisfied
even though I scratch until my skin is raw.

I can flirt but I can't order a coffee.
I can bargain but never close a deal.
I can convince someone that I don't belong
but not where I come from.

Tamil is a 25-year war with
no real winners
but plenty of statues of fallen soldiers
whose names no one remembers.

I have forgotten more Tamil than I ever knew.
My Tamil has never seen my parents kiss
but knows love isn't always something
you can witness.

My Tamil loves like the back of a hand
or a wooden spoon.
You only have to open the drawer
to where my Tamil lives
to get me to finally behave myself.

To say the word *Tamil* requires that you place
your tongue at the back of your mouth.
It is a different 'l' than loose and lewd and lovely,
three words my aunts use to describe
women like me.

My Tamil is always looking for a suitable boy.
My Tamil is always bragging about my job
but never my friendships.
The only thing my Tamil will always understand
about me is my desire to put an ocean between us.

Late

My father is a time-zone
on the other side of the globe,
always behind,
without a hope of catching up.
For someone whose livelihood
depends on making careful calculations
the math of time has always been
surprisingly just out of his reach,
like subway doors closing just as he reaches
the bottom of the stairs.

My nephew's high school graduation ceremony
has started.
Everyone is already seated and there is a slideshow
of cherubic baby photos superimposed
with teenagers eager to escape the confines
of their nine-to-three-thirty high school routine.
The principal is calling the grads
to receive their diplomas.
She is rapid-fire moving through the alphabet,
almost through the Bs,
and he tumbles into the seat beside me
at the last moment, grinning,
a third-base runner sliding into home plate,
declared safe.
The last three graduation programs in his hand,
the ones my mother and I had missed at the door,
rushing to get to our seats.

There is a sickly-sweet scent in the air, cologne,
which he is painstakingly dabbing
on a face he started shaving ten minutes
before we are supposed to be at dinner.

My mother patiently waits by the door,
in a red and gold embroidered sari
that she folded and draped for forty-five minutes
to achieve perfect pleats,
heavy dangling earrings that she had to coax
into her earlobes with a bit of soapy water,
a necklace made of individual gold coins
around her neck,
all turned to face the same direction.
She has taken time to do all of this
and somehow she is still waiting for my father.
I have time to count the gold coins
on her necklace,
to add extra pins to her pleats,
to sit in comfort of her baby powder
and Oil of Olay smell for a few minutes longer.

My father shows up late
to his brother-in-law's wake, paper plates
containing crumbs of mutton rolls and cake,
already served and eaten.
The people who came to pay respects are gone.
My aunt's head is bowed,
but immediately raises at the sound
of heavy footsteps breaking the silence,
sudden and booming,
like a grandfather clock striking midnight
in a sleepy house.
Her brave face crumples
at the sight of her older brother
as she finally allows herself to give in to tears.
He is right on time
to hold the heavy weight of her grief on his chest,
enveloping her in his arms like a final eulogy.

Some things are out of place

Like Billy Elliot's grandmother on her tiptoes,
teetering and unsteady, declaring
I could have been a dancer,
my *ammama* could have been a designer.

Instead of kneeling on an earthen floor
under a roof pockmarked
with holes from bombs, marking out a dress
for my 8-year-old frame,

if she had only stayed with us longer
than two short months of ceasefire
she would have missed the worst part of the war
and worked with something more beautiful

than thin, cheap cotton fabric.
A rich, off-the-shoulder blue velvet brocade,
perhaps with flowers woven together
with memories from a luxurious

comfortable life carefully stitched into the skirt.
How she would have marvelled at the ocean
so similar to her shores at home,
but more inviting somehow,

as she poked her sandalled feet
into the whitewash she would picture herself
swimming through waves, cresting and breaking,
how my *ammama* would have

closed her eyes and hummed along
as I played the piano,
an instrument she would never
have tired of if she had only heard it.

Buried her face into the lavender bushes
growing in our backyard instead of
into her hands, her eyes lighting up
and casting out the dark at the sunrise on the top

of the mountain behind our house,
something she had only seen in photographs.
When I say that
my *ammama* could have been a designer

I mean that she could fill vases with roses
even though nothing grows during the war.

Lately, I have been contemplating marriage

Did you know that Hindu brides wear red?
I ask, pulling your corset tight.
It symbolizes good luck and fertility.
Rather than walk down the aisle in white,
they shuffle, swaddled in metres of bright fabric.
I pin your veil to your head,
and you say with a laugh,
Suffocating! as I brace the strings,
your lace-covered flesh
protesting against the strain.

Instructions to ChatGPT in the year 2043

Write me a song that describes the pit in my stomach every time I pass him in the street with his new lover. Play it outside their window at 2am.

Describe a good wife. Roll a pie crust on the sidewalk in front of my apartment to show everyone what a good wife I would have made.

Give me the words to defend myself when I am accused of not trying hard enough, when in fact, I am not trying hard enough. Teach me to fight for what I want.

Explain why everyone loves me but no one is in love with me. In sonnet form.

Explain why I am more scared of being left at the altar than of spiders.

Explain the difference between a tremor in my heart and an earthquake.

Make me something tasty for lunch.

Make the bed.

Make the baby stop crying.

Make me stop crying.

Make me the kind of dancer people like to watch at weddings.

Make me a Tinder profile. Match with someone I will like. Go on the date for me. No, I don't care where you go to eat. No, I don't care what you wear. Yes, I am aware you can't actually go on a date for me. Yes, I am aware that I need to take more risks for love.

Blush when I walk into the room. Be spontaneous. Bring the romance back. Bring me marigolds every morning.

How to romance yourself
after Kait Quinn

Order yourself enough sushi for a small family
because you are your own small family. Ignore
that they have provided chopsticks for four
people. Bury your face in your cat's fur and
whisper your deepest secrets into her perfume. If
she claws you in the face it means she loves you.

Take yourself on a date to the farmers' market—
buy asparagus and free-range eggs with deep
sunflower yellow yolks so that you can eat brunch
on the floor of your kitchen and have your own
Italian Eat Pray Love moment. Buy yourself your
favorite flowers and tell yourself, *oh, you shouldn't
have*.

DM Pete Davidson.

Take yourself out for high tea, upgrade to the
extra fancy cucumber sandwiches, indulge in
scones with jam and full-fat clotted cream, stick
your pinky finger out when you sip your tea. Insist
on calling the man who serves you *garçon*.

Open your blinds and put on the uncensored
version of any Cardi B song. Make sure everyone
is watching. Dance like no one is watching.

Take a bubble bath with every essential oil and
bath bomb you can find. Invite the cat to join
you. If she claws you in the face, she is just

playing hard to get. Promise yourself that you'll never play hard to get with someone who loves you.

Let every work email that hopes to find you well find you lying in your hammock in the back yard sipping an Aperol spritz.

That evening, Netflix and chill, by yourself. Watch *Beauty and the Beast* under a weighted blanket. Finally admit to yourself that you found the Beast more attractive before he turned back into a prince.

Put on a matching pyjama set. Pick up your phone. Delete his number. Take a sexy selfie. Send it to your girlfriends.

Look at yourself in the mirror and say *I wish you were even more dramatic*. Whatever it is that you are made of you are not too much of it, you are just enough. You are not a side character. This is not someone else's story.

Untitled

Four eggs are fine
if you are making a Spanish omelette
but not if you are hoping to make a baby
with a man you haven't met yet.
As someone who not so secretly wants an A+
written on the top of any piece of paper
handed to me,
even if it is a just a receipt,
this number circled in red ink,
representing how many eggs the doctor managed
to coax from my reluctant ovaries,
makes me feel like she has just tattooed a C-
on my face.
I instantly compare myself to every woman
fifteen years younger than me
who is debating going off birth control,
whose body is full of promise
instead of question marks.
The doctor tells me it will take a few weeks for me
to feel normal again
but I haven't been feeling normal lately.
So I somehow find myself lying beside a lover
sooner than recommended,
his hand on my hip whispering
how sexy my engorged ovaries are.
And when he asks me *what does it feel like?*
I answer *it feels like buying a lottery ticket*
without getting to choose the numbers.
It feels like throwing pennies into an empty wishing well.
It feels like praying to a God, that no one really believes in.

What I did today instead of writing a poem

Googled *gestation period of an elephant.*

Despite not being an elephant, worried that my unborn child might belong to a terrible boyfriend that I recently broke up with. 7 years ago.

Googled *vaginal childbirth.*

Promptly threw my computer out the window.

Did a Kegel.

Watched a prenatal yoga video while eating a bowl of Doritos.

Did another Kegel.

Examined the 20-week ultrasound photos.

Worried that the baby doesn't look like me.

Texted my husband at work to ask if he *likes me as a friend or more than a friend.*

Went to the grocery store. Bought a 12-pack of Pepsi.

When the cashier asked me how far along I am, showed him my wedding ring and told him to stop flirting with me.

Went to the library. Checked out *Making More Milk*, *Breastfeeding Doesn't Need to Suck* and *Your Pregnancy After 35*.

Googled *geriatric pregnancy*. Read about all the risks associated with giving birth at 35. I'm 39.

Visited my geriatric parents.

Listened to my mom talk about how easy breastfeeding is.

Ate half a pound cake.

Ignored my mom when she asked when I last ate a vegetable.

Did another Kegel, discreetly.

Googled how big the baby should be by now.

Googled how big a sweet potato is.

Spent 30 minutes researching different varieties of sweet potato.

Roasted a sweet potato and called my mom to tell her that I am having vegetables for dinner.

A crown of sonnets for what to expect when you're expecting

If I hear about their babies once more
I'm not going to do anything but scream.
Maybe that will drown out the images.
A onesie, blue, pink or green, I don't care,
a breast coaxed into a ravenous mouth,
tiny hands curled around my fingertips,
lover's hands on my belly, whispering
look what our love made, our small miracle.
Our hearts on display outside our bodies.
My brown sugar skin with his pale blue eyes.
Without complaint, I swear I'd spend my nights
wide-eyed, still, watching her chest rise and fall.
I would rest easy knowing she's safe, but
all my friends say I'll never sleep again.

All my friends say I'll never sleep again.
But I'd give up my dreams in a heartbeat
if it means you get to keep yours. My child.
1 in 100. Those are the odds that
your tiny lungs and brain won't stand a chance.
If you were a flight we wouldn't risk it.
A gamble with no guaranteed winnings
but a 100% chance of me
crying at your birth. I would hold you close,
soothe your sobs, make you feel safe and wanted.
The doctor tells me not to panic yet
and not get my hopes up, but I'll love you
anyway, for as much time as we have.
A kiss, a hug, a lifetime, I'll take it.

A kiss, a hug, a lifetime, I'll take it.
I'll take you to prom, no date required.
No sleepovers, even if you scream that
I'm ruining your life, all I will hear
is *your life*. Coach you white-knuckled to dodge
a punch, a broken heart, boys in fast cars.
I'll teach you to drive, buy you your first thong.
You'll choose the cake flavour on my birthday.
I'll call you whatever name that you choose.
You, my surprise quiver in the belly,
a hurricane the size of a peanut.
Each kick a heart-shaped bruise. I take it back.
A sleepover anytime you want, for
as long as you live, as long as you live.

Five haiku

I stopped sucking in
not because I love me but
to make space for her.

When the baby kicks
I stroke my belly with a
soft it's never known.

I don't erase the
stretchmarks. They are proof that I
am growing with her.

What will she look like?
My husband says that for sure
she'll have a big nose.

Waxing my mustache
makes me tear up, but surely
hurts less than childbirth.

Acknowledgements

Thank you to the following publications for providing a home for some of the pieces that appear in this collection.

The poem *In this house we don't say I love you* first appeared in Issue 7 of Pensive.

The poem *Summer with my cousins, Scarborough (1992)* first appeared in a digital anthology published by Maza Arts Collective.

The poems *There is no mental illness in our family* and *Some things are out of place* first appeared in Fine Lines.

The poem *Questionnaire for potential partners* first appeared in Okay Donkey.

The poem *If you ask me if I'm fluent in Tamil* first appeared in Gnashing Teeth Publishing.

The poem *Late* first appeared in The Racket.

The poem *Lately I have been contemplating marriage* first appeared in a chapbook published by The Ontario Poetry Society.

The poem *How to romance yourself* first appeared in Quail Bell Magazine.

Many thanks

To the team at Garden of Neuro Publishing, especially Nanci Arvizu, for your enthusiasm and support in publishing this collection. Thank you for supporting women's writing, including mine.

To the members of the Victoria Poetry Project and anyone who has ever attended or graced the stage at an open mic at Caffe Fantastico, you have my gratitude for your audience and admiration for sharing your work.

To Megan Falley, for creating the Poems That Don't Suck course and an incredible community of poets with whom I have shared work, celebrated, commiserated, and always, continued to write.

To my friends who insist I am wasting my time working as a lawyer and should be a full-time poet, my mom disagrees with you but I bask in the sunshine of your compliments.

To my parents and sisters, for showing me how to be comfortable in my own skin by being comfortable in yours.

To Colin, the enthusiastic reader of my first drafts and subject of all my (happy) love poems. Thank you for always laughing at the right parts.

To Selvi, my inspiration from the womb and beyond. Thank you for choosing me.